SEASONS OF FUN: SPRING

SPRING SPORTS

by J. P. Press

Consultant: Beth Gambro
Reading Specialist, Yorkville, Illinois

Minneapolis, Minnesota

Teaching Tips

Before Reading

- Look at the cover of the book. Discuss the picture and the title.
- Ask readers to brainstorm a list of what they already know about spring sports. What can they expect to see in the book?
- Go on a picture walk, looking through the pictures to discuss vocabulary and make predictions about the text.

During Reading

- Read for purpose. Encourage readers to think about spring sports as they are reading.
- Ask readers to look for the details of the book. What is happening?
- If readers encounter an unknown word, ask them to look at the sounds in the word. Then, ask them to look at the rest of the page. Are there any clues to help them understand?

After Reading

- Encourage readers to pick a buddy and reread the book together.
- Ask readers to name three spring sports from the book. Go back and find the pages that tell about each sport.
- Ask readers to write or draw something they learned about spring sports.

Credits:

Cover and title page, © Bohbeh/Shutterstock, © photastic/Shutterstock, © pukach/Shutterstock, Dan Thornberg/Shutterstock, © azure1/Shutterstock; 3, © Gearstd/iStock; 5, © fstop123/iStock; 7, © rmanera/iStock; 8, © Peieq/iStock; 8–9, © Bwilson/Shutterstock; 10, © vlastas/iStock; 11, © Africa Studio/Shutterstock; 12–13, © SewCream/Shutterstock; 14, © ESB Professional/Shutterstock; 16, © WoodysPhotos/Shutterstock; 17, © Click Images/Shutterstock; 18, © CHRISTOPHE ROLLAND/Shutterstock; 19, © Denis Kuvaev/Shutterstock; 21, © FatCamera/iStock; 22T, © Sports Studio Photos/gettyimages; 22M, © Transcendental Graphics/gettyimages; 22B, © DarrenFisher/iStock; 23TL, © ithinksky/iStock, © Vitawin/Shutterstock; 23TM, © LSOphoto/iStock; 23TR, © RichVintage/iStock; 23BL, © DenKuvaiev/iStock; 23BM, © CDH_Design/iStock; 23BR, © mediaphotos/iStock.

Library of Congress Cataloging-in-Publication Data

Names: Press, J. P., 1995- author.
Title: Spring sports / by J. P. Press ; Consultant: Beth Gambro, Reading
   Specialist, Yorkville, Illinois.
Description: Minneapolis, Minnesota : Bearport Publishing Company, [2022] |
   Series: Seasons of fun: spring | Includes bibliographical references and index.
Identifiers: LCCN 2021030919 (print) | LCCN 2021030920 (ebook) | ISBN
   9781636913971 (library binding) | ISBN 9781636914022 (paperback) | ISBN
   9781636914077 (ebook)
Subjects: LCSH: Sports--Juvenile literature. | Spring--Juvenile literature.
Classification: LCC GV705.4 .P73 2022 (print) | LCC GV705.4 (ebook) | DDC
   796--dc23
LC record available at https://lccn.loc.gov/2021030919
LC ebook record available at https://lccn.loc .gov/2021030920

Copyright © 2022 Bearport Publishing Company. All rights reserved. No part of this publication may be reproduced in whole or in part, stored in a retrieval system, or transmitted in any form or by any means, electronic, mechanical, photocopying, recording, or otherwise, without written permission from the publisher.

For more information, write to Bearport Publishing, 5357 Penn Avenue South, Minneapolis, MN 55419. Printed in the United States of America.

Contents

Playing Sports 4

The History of Baseballs 22

Glossary 23

Index 24

Read More 24

Learn More Online 24

About the Author 24

Playing Sports

It is time for spring fun!

There are many sports to play in the spring.

Which sport will I play?

Baseball is fun in the spring.

I swing the **bat**.

Crack!

The ball goes flying.

I hit a home run!

My sister plays softball.

She throws the big, yellow ball to **home plate**.

The ball goes so fast!

Home plate

Soccer is another fun sport.

I like to kick the ball hard.

Let's go play soccer at the park.

When we are done,
let's grab our **rackets**.

It is time for tennis.

We hit the ball over
a net.

Golf is fun, too.

First, we hit the ball really far.

Then, we tap it softly into the hole.

My friend plays lacrosse in the spring.

Wearing a **helmet** and **pads** keeps him safe.

My friend shoots at the net.

He scores!

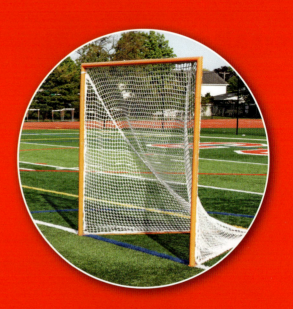

At school, I do track and field.

I am on the part of the team that does **jumping**.

My friend runs on the track.

Spring sports are so much fun!

I want to try them all.

Which spring sport do you like best?

21

The History of Baseballs

The first baseballs were made in the 1800s. They were all different. Some were made from old shoes. Some were even made with fish eyes!

Later, baseballs got bigger and heavier. But they were still made of many different things.

Now, all baseballs are the same. They are the same size and made of the same things. Let's play ball!

Glossary

bat a wooden or metal stick used to hit a baseball or softball

helmet a hard hat worn to keep the head safe

home plate the spot on a baseball or softball field where people stand to bat

jumping a sport where people try to jump the farthest or highest

pads things worn to keep the body safe

rackets frames with handles and strings used to hit tennis balls

Index

baseball 6, 22
golf 15
lacrosse 16
soccer 10
softball 8
tennis 12
track and field 18

Read More

Carr, Aaron. *Tennis (Like a Pro).* New York: AV2, 2020.

Meister, Cari. *Softball Fun (Sports Fun).* North Mankato, MN: Capstone Press, 2021.

Learn More Online

1. Go to **www.factsurfer.com** or scan the QR code below.
2. Enter "**Spring Sports**" into the search box.
3. Click on the cover of this book to see a list of websites.

About the Author

J. P. Press likes running. She looks forward to the first run in shorts every spring.